Take a trip to
NORWAY

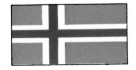

Keith Lye
General Editor
Henry Pluckrose

Franklin Watts

London   New York   Sydney   Toronto

Facts about Norway

Area:
324,219 sq. km.
(125,182 sq. miles)

Population:
4,148,000 (1984 estimate)

Capital:
Oslo

Largest cities:
Oslo (450, 000);
Bergen (207,000);
Trondheim (135,000);
Stavanger (91,000)

Official language:
Norwegian

Religion:
Christianity
(Evangelical Lutheran
Church)

Main exports:
Oil and gas, machinery
and transport equipment,
metals and metal products

Currency:
Krone

Franklin Watts Limited
12a Golden Square
London W1

ISBN: UK Edition 0 86313 211 1
ISBN: US Edition 0 531 04885 3
Library of Congress Catalog
Card No: 84–51508

© Franklin Watts Limited 1984

Typeset by Ace Filmsetting Ltd,
Frome, Somerset
Printed in Hong Kong

Text Editor: Brenda Williams

Maps: Edward Kinsey

Design: Edward Kinsey

Stamps: Stanley Gibbons Limited

Photographs: Zefa; J. Allan Cash, 6, 7,
23, 24, 25, 26, 27, 28, 30, 31
Front cover: J. Allan Cash
Back cover: Zefa

The Kingdom of Norway is a large country in northwest Europe. It was covered by ice during the Ice Age which ended about 10,000 years ago. Ice rivers, called glaciers, wore out deep valleys. Many such valleys are now sea inlets called fiords. This is Geirangerfiord in central Norway.

Glaciers are still found in Norway's mountains. The second largest glacier is named Svartisan and lies near Moi i Rana, in northern Norway. Ice melts at the bottom of glaciers and the water flows away in rivers.

A third of Norway lies north of the Arctic Circle. Here – in the Land of the Midnight Sun – the Sun does not set for at least one day a year. This picture was taken near Tromsø, where the Midnight Sun shines from May 21 to July 23.

Norway is a monarchy. King Olav
V became king in 1957 and lives at
the Royal Palace in Oslo, the capital
city. Norway was joined with
Denmark from 1380 to 1814. In 1815,
it was joined with Sweden. But in
1905, Norway at last elected its own
king.

The country's parliament, called the Storting, makes Norway's laws. Everyone over 18 years of age can vote to elect its members. The parliament building is also in Oslo.

The picture shows some stamps and money used in Norway. The main unit of currency is the krone, which contains 100 ore.

WORLD
MAP

Norway

North Cape

•Hammerfest

LAPLAND

•Tromsø

Lofoten
Islands

•Narvik

Arctic Circle

•Bodo
▲Svartisan

NORWEGIAN
SEA

Trondheim•

Kristiansund•

SWEDEN

FINLAND

▲2469

NORWAY

•Granvin

Oslo•

Bergen•

Drammen•

•Skien

Stavanger•

•Kristiansand

Skagerrak

BALTIC
SEA

9

In northern Norway, Sweden and Finland is a treeless region called Lapland. The Lapps were once nomads, who wandered about following herds of reindeer. They lived in canvas tents, which had an opening to let out smoke.

The 20,000 Lapps who live in northern Norway are called Samer. Today, many no longer live a wandering life in tents. Instead, they have modern homes in farming and fishing villages.

Oslo is in southeast Norway.
Most Norwegians are fair-haired and
have blue eyes. Their language has
two forms. Bokmål is like Danish and
is the official written language.
Landsmål, or Nynorsk, is made up of
various Norwegian dialects.

Bergen is Norway's second largest city. It is in the southwest and is important for fishing and industry. Bergen has a mild climate, with January temperatures of 2°C (36°F) and July temperatures of 17°C (63°F). Western Norway is warmed by the waters of the North Atlantic Drift.

Trondheim, the third largest city, is in westcentral Norway. It was once the country's capital. The great Nidaros Cathedral dates from the 11th century and is one of the finest churches in northern Europe.

Between the 9th and 11th centuries,
sea-farers called Vikings set out from
Norway, Denmark and Sweden.
They sailed in longships, like this one
in a museum near Oslo. Vikings
raided many places in Europe, but
they also founded settlements in
Iceland and Greenland, and explored
the coasts of North America.

In a museum near Oslo is a balsa-wood raft called the *Kon-Tiki*. This was built in 1947 by the Norwegian adventurer Thor Heyerdahl, who sailed it from Peru to eastern Polynesia. He showed that the people who first settled in Polynesia may also have sailed from South America.

Oslo is the base for the country's merchant ships. The Norwegian fleet is one of the world's biggest. It earns much money for Norway by carrying goods from one country to another.

Little of Norway's land can be farmed. One farming area is around Oslo, even though this region has a harsher climate than the southwest. Other farm areas are around Kristiansund and Trondheim. Crops include barley, hay and oats.

About 35,000 people in Norway earn their living from fishing. Cod fishing is important in the hilly Lofoten Islands of the northwest. The scenery of the Lofoten Islands also attracts many tourists.

Hammerfest is Europe's most northerly town. Here the Sun does not set from May 17 to July 28, nor does it rise between November 21 and January 23. But Hammerfest is an ice-free port, warmed by the North Atlantic Drift as it flows from the Caribbean Sea.

Much of Norway is barren, but forests of pine, spruce and other trees cover about a third of the land. Timber from the forests is used to make wood pulp and paper. Many farm houses are made of wood.

Stavanger, in the southwest, is the home of Norway's oil and natural gas industry. The oil and gas are taken from the bed of the North Sea through oil-rigs like the one being built here. Norway also mines copper, iron ore, lead and zinc.

Out of every 100 workers in Norway, 7 work in farming, fishing and forestry. Another 37 have jobs in industry. Nearly all of Norway's electricity is made by water power at hydroelectric stations, such as here near Geilo. Much of the electricity is used in factories.

Iron ore is carried by rail from the rich mines at Kiruna, in Sweden. It comes to Narvik, an ice-free port in northern Norway. The ore is then shipped to other countries through Narvik's port.

Coal is mined and sent abroad
from Spitsbergen, one of the
Norwegian Svalbard Islands in the
Arctic Ocean. The Russians also
have coal mines on these islands.

Norway is one of Europe's richest countries and the people enjoy a high standard of living. These Norwegians are staying at the resort of Granvin in the Hardangerfiord, east of Bergen.

Norwegians enjoy buffet meals called the koldtbord, or cold table. They include cold meats, shrimps, salted herring and other fish, cheese, tomatoes, lettuce and various breads.

Education in Norway is free and children between the ages of 7 and 16 must attend school. Many then go on to upper secondary schools. This modern primary school is at the port of Bodø, in northern Norway.

Skiing and ice-skating are popular winter sports. At the huge Holmen-kollen ski jump near Oslo, a Ski Festival is held every year. Boating, climbing, fishing, soccer and swimming are popular summer pastimes.

Norway's National Theatre in Oslo was built in the 1890s. The country's most famous playwright was Henrik Ibsen. One of his plays was Peer Gynt. Music for it was written by Edvard Grieg, Norway's best-known composer.

Norway's mountains and fiords are among Europe's most beautiful scenery. But the country has few people. Tourism, especially cruising along the coasts, is important. These ships are in the magnificent Geirangerfiord.

Index

Arctic Circle 5

Bergen 13
Bodø 28

Coal 25
Climate 13, 20

Education 28

Farming 20
Fishing 18–19
Food 26–27
Forestry 21

Geirangerfiord 3, 31
Glaciers 3–4
Government 11

Hammerfest 18
Hardangerfiord 26
Heyerdahl, Thor 16
History 10, 15
Holmenkollen Ski Festival 29
Hydroelectricity 22

Industry 22

Kon-Tiki 16

Language 12
Lapland 6–7
Lofoten Islands 19

Midnight Sun 5
Money 8

Narvik 24
National Theatre 30

Oil rig 23
Oslo 10–11, 12, 17, 29–30

Pastimes 29

Royal Palace 10

Schools 28
Skiing 29
Spitsbergen 25
Stamps 8
Stavanger 23
Storting 11
Svalbard Islands 25
Svartisan glacier 4

Trondheim 14

Vikings 15